Growing Readers

Purchased with Smart Start Funds

Seeing

by Helen Frost

Consulting Editor: Gail Saunders-Smith, Ph.D.

Consultant: Eric H. Chudler, Ph.D.
Research Associate Professor
Department of Anesthesiology
University of Washington, Seattle

Pebble Books

an imprint of Capstone Press
Mankato, Minnesota

Pebble Books are published by Capstone Press
818 North Willow Street, Mankato, Minnesota 56001
http://www.capstone-press.com

Library of Congress Cataloging-in-Publication Data
Frost, Helen, 1949–
Seeing/by Helen Frost.
    p. cm.—(The senses)
    Includes bibliographical references and index.
    Summary: Simple text and photographs present the sense of seeing and how
it works.
    ISBN 0-7368-0383-1
    1. Vision—Juvenile literature. [1. Vision. 2. Eye. 3. Senses and sensation.]
I. Title. II. Series: Frost, Helen, 1949– The senses.
QP475.7.F76 2000
612.8'4—dc21   99-18968
                                                                                    CIP

Note to Parents and Teachers

The Senses series supports national science standards for units related to behavioral science. This book describes and illustrates the sense of sight. The photographs support early readers in understanding the text. The repetition of words and phrases helps early readers learn new words. This book also introduces early readers to subject-specific vocabulary words, which are defined in the Words to Know section. Early readers may need assistance to read some words and to use the Table of Contents, Words to Know, Read More, Internet Sites, and Index/Word List sections of the book.

Table of Contents

Sight is one of your five senses. You see with your eyes.

iris

pupil

6

You can see the front parts of eyes. The iris is the colored part. The pupil is the dark circle in the iris.

Light rays bounce off objects you see. Light rays go into your pupils.

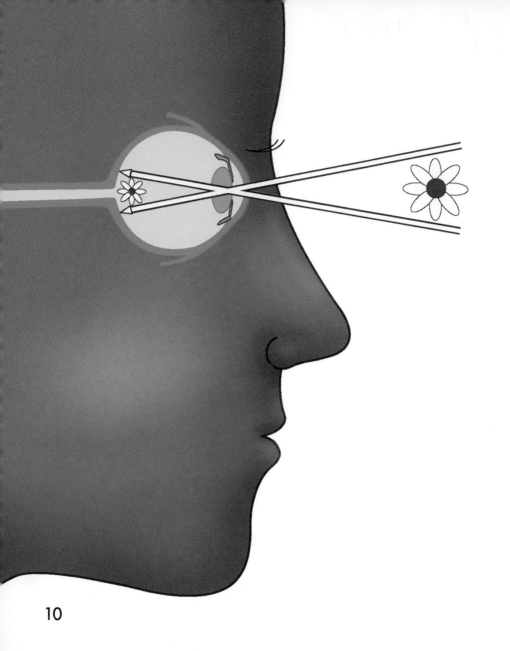

Light rays make a picture on the back of your eyes. Your eyes send signals to your brain. Your brain understands what your eyes see.

Everything looks gray in dim light. You can see only shapes.

14

You can see better in bright light. You can see shapes and colors.

Your eyes see many colors. Your brain understands the colors you see.

18

Objects far away look small. Objects close up look big. Your eyes and brain tell you how far away things are.

Your sense of sight
tells you about things
around you. It tells
you about their sizes,
shapes, and colors.

Words to Know

brain—the body part inside your head that controls your body; your brain understands what your eyes see.

iris—the colored part of your eye; most people's irises are blue, green, brown, or gray; the iris controls the amount of light allowed into your eye.

pupil—the dark center of your eye; your pupils let light into your eyes; your pupils get larger in dim light to let in more light; your pupils get smaller in bright light to let in less light.

ray—a narrow beam of light; rays of light bounce off objects and go into your pupils.

sense—a way of knowing about things around you; sight is one of your five senses; hearing, smelling, tasting, and touching are your other senses.

Read More

Ballard, Carol. *How Do Our Eyes See?* How Your Body Works. Austin, Texas: Raintree Steck-Vaughn, 1998.

Hurwitz, Sue. *Sight.* The Library of the Five Senses and the Sixth Sense. New York: PowerKids Press, 1997.

Pluckrose, Henry Arthur. *Looking and Seeing.* Senses. Austin, Texas: Raintree Steck-Vaughn, 1998.

Internet Sites

Anatomy of the Eye
http://www.eyenet.org/public/anatomy/anatomy.html

Sense of Sight
http://www.yucky.com/body/index.ssf?/systems/sight/

Sight
http://faculty.washington.edu/chudler/chvision.html

Index/Word List

big, 19
brain, 11, 17, 19
bright, 15
circle, 7
close up, 19
color, 15, 17, 21
colored, 7
dark, 7
dim, 13
eyes, 5, 7, 11, 17, 19

far away, 19
front, 7
iris, 7
light, 13, 15
light rays, 9, 11
objects, 9, 19
picture, 11
pupil, 7, 9
see, 5, 7, 9, 11, 13, 15, 17
send, 11
sense, 5, 21

shape, 13, 15, 21
sight, 5, 21
signals, 11
size, 21
small, 19
understands, 11, 17

Word Count: 149
Early-Intervention Level: 15

Editorial Credits
Mari C. Schuh, editor; Timothy Halldin, cover designer; Kevin T. Kes and Linda Clavel illustrators; Kimberly Danger, photo researcher

Photo Credits
David F. Clobes, 18 (both)
Gregg R. Andersen, 12, 14
Photo Network, 8; Photo Network/Peter Fownes, 1
Photophile/Robert W. Ginn, 4
Tom Stack/TOM STACK & ASSOCIATES, 6
Uniphoto, 20; Uniphoto/Ed Elberfeld, cover
Visuals Unlimited/Mark E. Gibson, 16